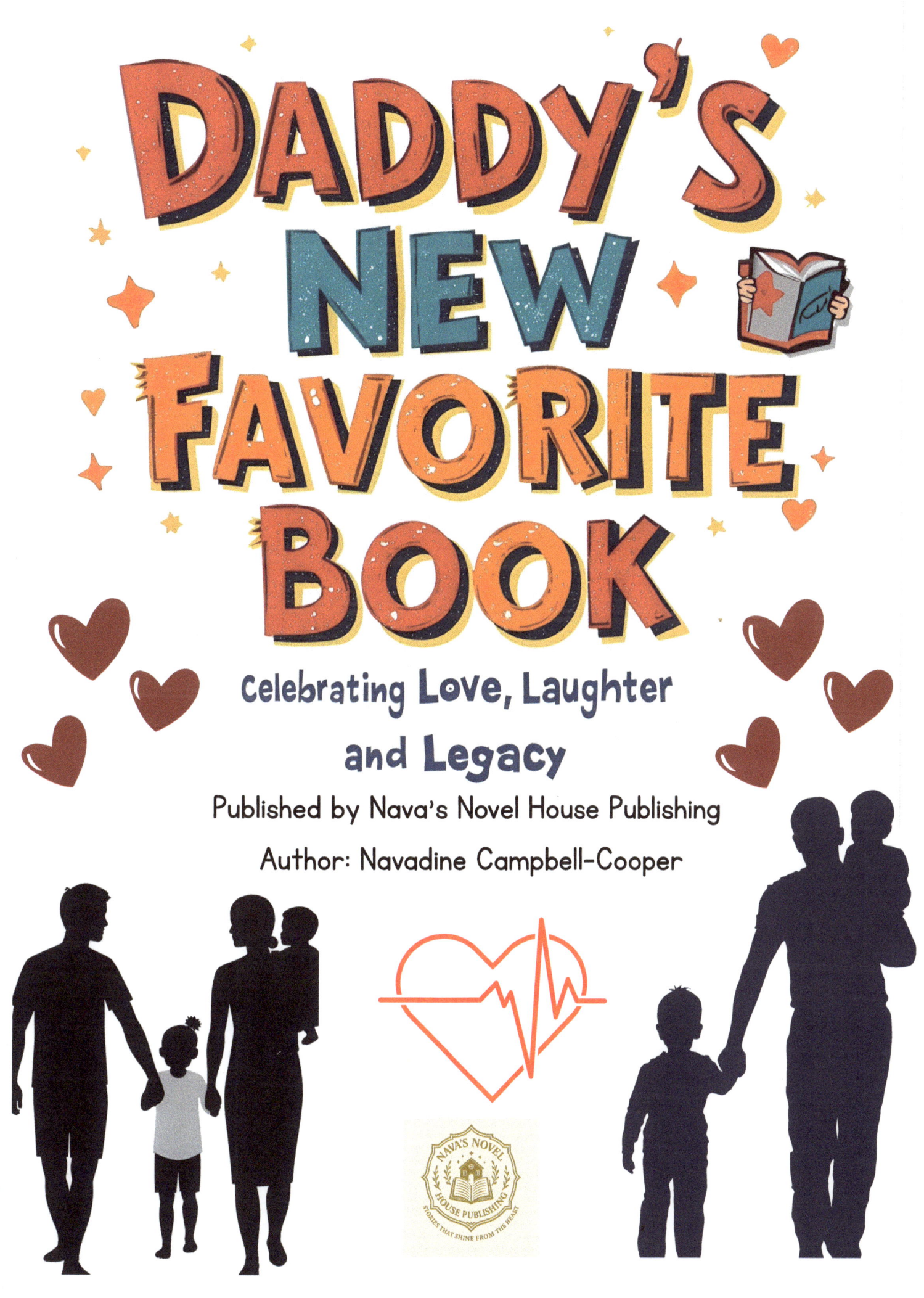

THIS BOOK BELONGS TO:

_____

(write your dad's name)

Dad and All of Us

Copyright Page

Daddy's New Favorite Book:
Celebrating Love, Laughter, and Legacy

© 2025 Navadine Campbell-Cooper

All rights reserved.
No part of this publication may be reproduced, distributed, or transmitted in any form or by any means, including photocopying, recording, or other electronic or mechanical methods, without the prior written permission of the publisher, except in the case of brief quotations embodied in reviews and certain other noncommercial uses permitted by copyright law.

Published by:
Nava's Novel House Publishing
Tucson, Arizona, USA

ISBN:979-8-9935052-0-6

Printed in the United States of America
First Edition, 2025

Acknowledgments

To my husband, Joseph — thank you for being the heart behind every story, and for inspiring this book through your laughter, patience, and love as a father.

To our son, Akrit — your giggles, cuddles, and curiosity make every day a new chapter of joy. You are the reason I write with love.

To every dad reading this — thank you for showing up, for the bedtime stories, the bear hugs, and the moments that make childhood magical.

And to God, for blessing me with the gift of family and the words to honor them.

HAPPY FATHER'S *Day*

Dedicated to All Dads,
My first hero, my forever friend.
The one who makes bedtime stories,
bear hugs, and belly laughs the best
part of every day.
Thank you for the laughter, the
lessons, and the love you share always.
With love, always and forever.

A Father's Day Gift from _____,
_____, _____, and _____.
A Dad we wouldn't change for the world, our superhero, Our true love!

Dear Daddy,
We made this book for you—
with tiny hands, big love,
and a whole bunch of glue!

_____ loves your shoulder rides,

_____ says you're super wise,

_____ cheers when you cook your stew,

_____ loves tickles, just from you!

Sketch a Favorite Memory with Pad

Best Dad Ever

You fix what's broken, calm our fears,
Catch our giggles, wipe our tears.
You carry our hearts in your steady hands,
And love in ways no one else understands.

Some dads might fly or wear a cape,
But you're the one who helps us shape our dreams, our joy, and who we'll be—
With you, we become who we're meant to be

When we're wild, you stay so calm,
When we fall, you're there like balm.
You teach us to be brave and true—
We all want to grow up just like you.

You read with voices that make us laugh,
You fill our nights with stories and baths,
We splash, then snuggle — one last hooray,
With Daddy, it's the best end to our day.

You play with us and make us grin,
While Mommy cooks and joins right in.
Our home is filled with laughter's tune,
Our hearts with love so warm and true.
Each day's an adventure, thanks to you.

So here's a gift to celebrate you—
A story stitched in hugs times two!
From _____, _____, _____, and _____ too,
This book says: "We really LOVE YOU!"

Here's our favorite picture of us—
A moment you can always trust,
To remind you how much we care,
With you, we become who we're meant to be.

Our favorite Picture of Us

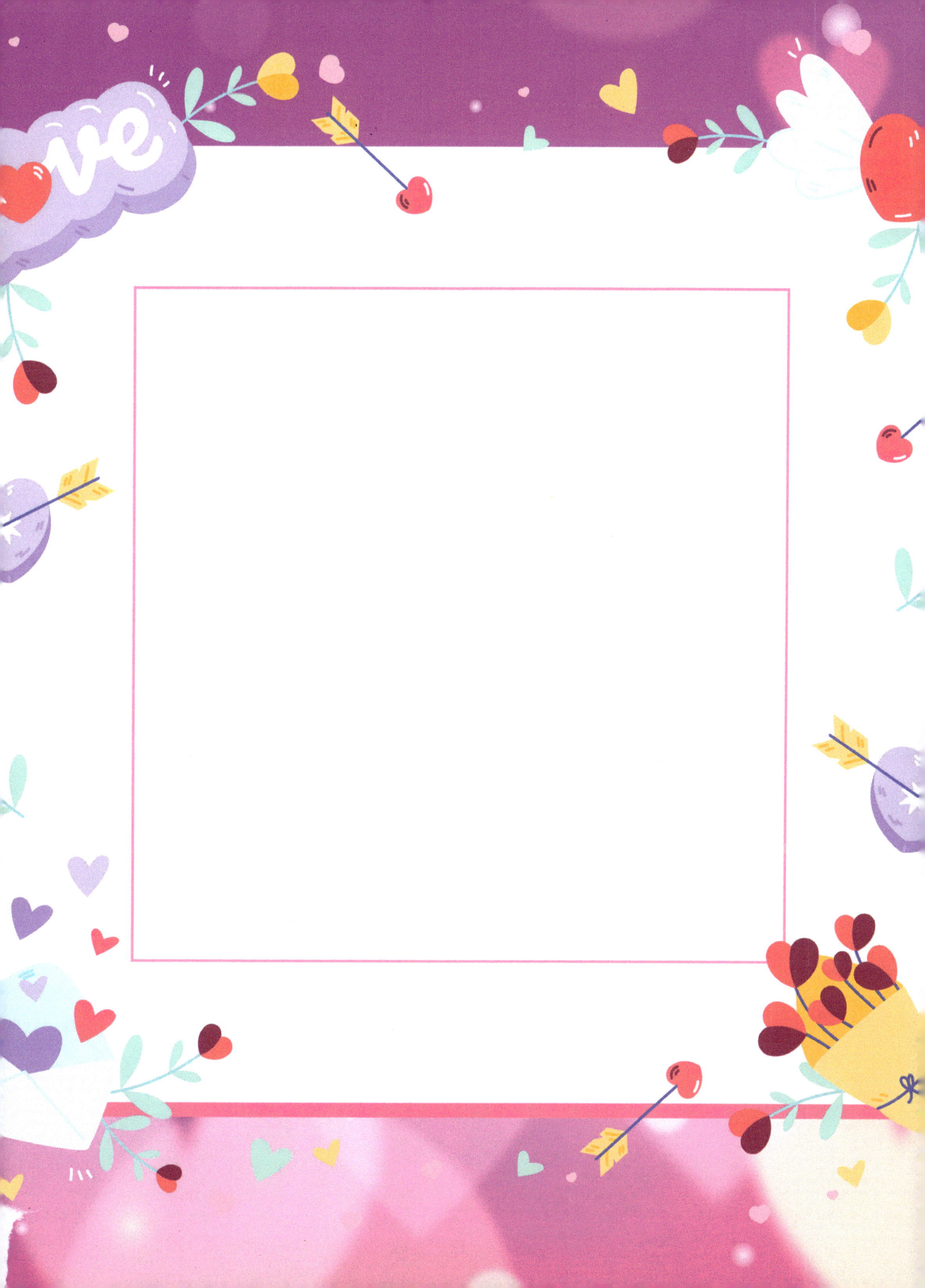

Happy Father's Day, Daddy!
We love you more than bath time bubbles,
basketball games, and bedtime snuggles.
Love,
_____, _____, _____, and _____
Now, let's look back at our favorite moments with Dad.

You play all our games, even when you're tired,
You cheer the loudest when we feel inspired.
Whether tag, hide-and-seek, or jumping so high,
You're our favorite teammate — the best of them all!

You help with our snacks, our spills, and our shoes,
Even on days when you've got work to do.
You're the one we run to when things go wrong,
With hugs and advice that help us stay strong.

You show up for birthdays, for games, and for plays,
Even when traffic or work gets in the way.
You make time for us, and that means the most.
Of all the dads, we'd pick you, hands down, no boast!

Some days we argue or make a big mess,
But you handle it all with calm and finesse.
You teach us to try, to talk things through,
And we're learning a lot just by watching you.

So we made this book with love from us four,
Because you're the Daddy that we all adore.
It's laughter, it's hugs, it's memories made,
And this is your favorite book — with love that won't fade.

Our Special Moment

(Place your favorite photo here)

Write your favorite memory with Dad here:

_____

_____

_____

Draw A Picture of You and Dad- Doing Something Fun Together

Our Favorite Adventure Together

A special Note to Daddy

_____

_____

A Special Dedication

This book is lovingly dedicated to

_____
_____
_____
_____
_____
_____
_____
_____
_____
_____
_____
_____
_____
_____
_____.

With love from: _____

A Special Dedication

This book is lovingly dedicated to

_____

_____

_____

_____

_____

_____

_____

_____

_____

_____

_____

_____

_____

_____ .

With love from: _____

What makes Daddy special?

A Message for Daddy

Dear Daddy,

You've taught me that love is patient, laughter is powerful, and family is forever.

When I grow up, I'll remember your hugs, your jokes, and the way your eyes light up when you see me smile.

Thank you for being my greatest adventure and my favorite story to read again and again.

Love always,
_____

Happy Father's Day!

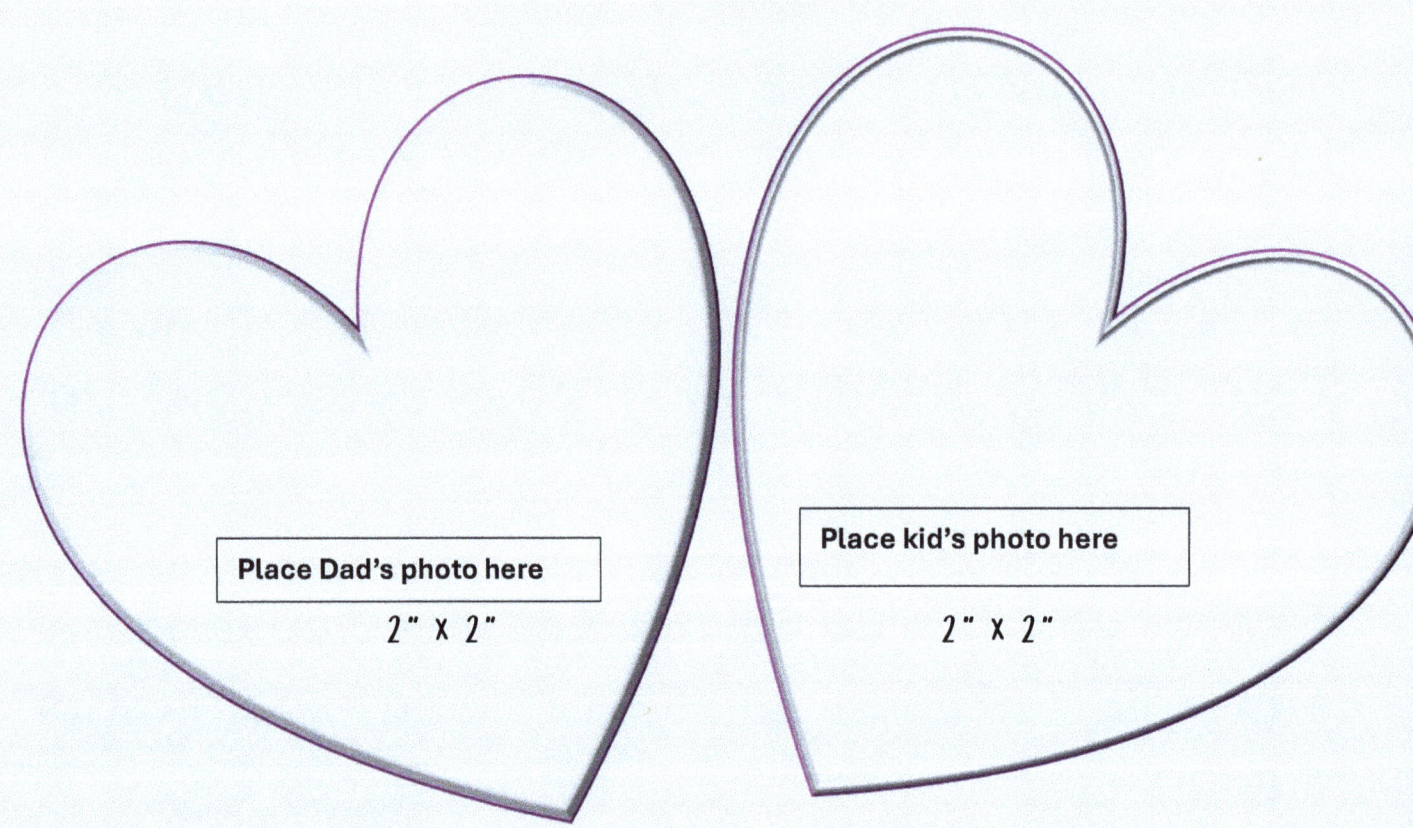

Place Dad's photo here 2" x 2"

Place kid's photo here 2" x 2"

I love you because you are our one and only dad!

Who needs a superhero when we have you!
   This book was gifted to Daddy by_____ on _____.

LOVE: _____

Daddy's New Favorite Book

Celebrating Love, Laughter and Legacy

Published by Nava's Novel House Publishing

Author: Navadine Campbell-Cooper

ABOUT THE AUTHOR

Navadine Campbell-Cooper is a teacher, wife, mother, and author who believes the greatest stories begin at home. Her books capture the laughter, love, and legacy shared between parents and their children, transforming ordinary moments into timeless keepsakes.

Through Nava's Novel House Publishing, Navadine creates heartfelt works that celebrate family, faith, and the simple joys of childhood. Each page she writes is inspired by her own journey as a wife and mother, and by the enduring love that continues to shape her family's story.

With each book, readers are encouraged to shine from their hearts and share love generously.

Nava's Novel House Publishing seeks to inspire tomorrow's generation to be bold, kind, and courageous—touching one heart at a time and nurturing future leaders to be their very best.

Published by

Nava's Novel House Publishing
Tucson, Arizona, U.S.A.

www.ingramcontent.com/pod-product-compliance
Lightning Source LLC
Chambersburg PA
CBHW041217130526
44582CB00026BA/90